Starfish
K3
Student's Book

> Catalogue Publication Data

Starfish K3 Student's Book
Author: Angela Llanas, Libby Williams
Pearson Educación de México, S.A. de C.V., 2019
ISBN: 978-607-32-4664-4
Area: ELT
Format: 30.5 x 23.5 cm   Page count: 248

Managing Director: Sergio Fonseca ■ **Innovation & Learning Delivery Director:** Alan David Palau ■ **Regional Content Manager - English:** Andrew Starling ■ **Publisher:** Hened Manzur ■ **Content Development:** Catalina Hernandez ■ **Content Support:** Canda Machado ■ **Art and Design Coordinator:** Juan Manuel Santamaría ■ **Design Process Supervisor:** Salvador Pereira ■ **Layout:** Berenice Hinojosa ■ **Cover Design:** BrandB/Fenómeno ■ **Interior Design:** BrandB/Fenómeno ■ **Photo Research:** Salvador Pereira ■ **Photo Credits:** Shutterstock ■ **Illustrations:** Ana Elena García, Gerardo Sánchez, Miguel Ángel Chávez, Herenia González, Ismael Vázquez, José de Santiago Torices, Marcela Gómez, Mónica Cahué, Olivia González, Sergio Salto, Sheila Cabeza de Vaca, Tania Dinorah Recio, Víctor Sandoval, Ximena García Trigos

The Publisher wishes to acknowledge the valuable collaboration of **Sophie Angerman**, author of the Mathematics program.

© Pearson Educación de México, S.A. de C.V., 2019

First published, 2019

ISBN PRINT BOOK: 978-607-32-4664-4

D.R. © 2019 por Pearson Educación de México, S.A. de C.V.
Avenida Antonio Dovalí Jaime #70
Torre B, Piso 6, Colonia Zedec Ed. Plaza Santa Fe
Delegación Álvaro Obregón, México, Ciudad de México, C. P. 01210

Esta obra se terminó de imprimir en enero del 2023, en los talleres de Servicios Profesionales de Impresión S.A. de C.V.
Calle Mimosas 31, Col. Santa María Insurgentes, C. P. 06430
México, CDMX

www.pearsonelt.com

Impreso en México. *Printed in Mexico.*

1 2 3 4 5 6 7 8 9 0 - 22 21 20 19

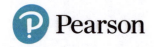

All rights reserved. No part of this publication may be reproduced, stored in a retrieval system, or transmitted in any form or by any means, electronic, mechanical, photocopying, recording, or otherwise, without the prior permission of the publisher.

Pearson Hispanoamérica
Argentina ■ Belice ■ Bolivia ■ Chile ■ Colombia ■ Costa Rica ■ Cuba ■ República Dominicana ■ Ecuador ■ El Salvador ■ Guatemala ■ Honduras ■ México ■ Nicaragua ■ Panamá ■ Paraguay ■ Perú ■ Uruguay ■ Venezuela

Contents

Unit		Page
1	Who do you like to play with?	4
2	What parts of your body help you feel?	29
3	Why is your family important to you?	54
4	What happens to your body when you are hot or cold?	79
5	Why is it important to take care of our planet?	116
6	How can you stay healthy?	141
7	How can you take care of animals?	178
8	Which is your favorite place in town?	203

Unit 1 Who do you like to play with?

- Are you happy or sad when you play with your friends? Color.

- **Listen, read, and say who they are.**

She is...  He is...

- **Check the things the children are going to see at school.**

a new classroom

a new teacher

new friends

Objectives: Make predictions about a story.

Unit 1

- Trace and say.

M m

- Listen. Cut and paste.

milk   mangoes   milk and mangoes

Objectives: Identify the /m/ sound.

- **Say and color.**

Mathematical Thinking

Learning to Know

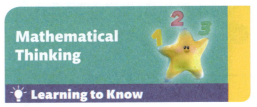 square

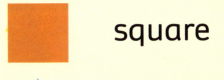 rhombus

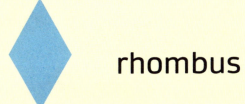 circle

 trapezoid

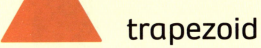 hexagon

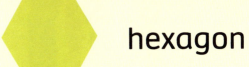 triangle

Objectives: Identify basic shapes.

- **Listen and number the pictures in order.**

Language Instruction and Communication
Learning to Know

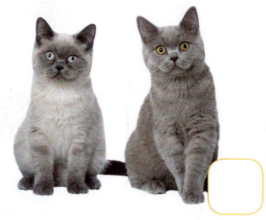

- **Draw your picture. Compare it with a friend's.**

Unit 1

Objectives: Describe their physical characteristics and those of others.

- **Listen and circle the activities children do in school in the USA.** 🎧 ✏️

- **Look and circle the things you do in your classroom.**

Think!
What do you do to keep your classroom clean and organized?

Objectives: Learn to take care of things at school.

- **Draw 😊 for the kind comment. Draw 😢 for the unkind comment.** ✏️

"Do you like my drawing?"

"I like it. It's beautiful!"

"I don't like it. It's awful!"

- **Draw a picture and share it with the class. Make kind comments.**

Unit 1

Objectives: Express likes and dislikes.

- **Listen and read. Circle their imaginary friend.**

Mitzi, Max, and Sasha

- **Trace and say.**

S s

- **Listen and match. Trace the words.**

snake

stop

sleep

- **Listen, act, and sing.**

Objectives: Identify the /s/ sound.

- **Complete the sequences.**

| 14 | 15 | 16 | | 18 | | 20 | 21 |

| 2 | | 4 | | 6 | | 8 | |

| 21 | 22 | | 24 | | 26 | | 28 |

- **Complete the patterns.**

- **Match the faces with the children.**

Language Instruction and Communication
Learning to Know

- **Listen and trace the words.**

happy　　sad　　angry　　excited　scared

Unit 1

Objectives: Talk about different feelings and why they are important.

- **Listen and match the children to their countries.**

Exploration and Knowing of the World
Learning to Do

Mariana

Seth

- **Listen and circle the correct answer.**

Her name is Maria / Mariana.

She is 5 / 6 years old.

She likes / doesn't like school.

Objectives: Identify new people at school and find out who they are.

Unit 1

- **Look and say why Sandra is sad.**

- **Draw a self-esteem portrait.**
- **Share and say why you are happy.**

Objectives: Express how they feel by using target language.

● **Listen and number the pictures in order.**

Mitzi and Max Get It Right

- Listen and chant.

- Listen, trace, and draw.

mom   man   mat

Objectives: Identify the /m/ sound.

- **Complete the calendar.**

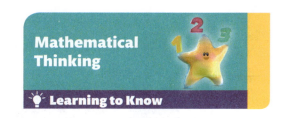

September 2019

Sunday	Monday	Tuesday	Wednesday	Thursday	Friday	Saturday
1	2 ⭐				6 ⭐	
				12	13	
						21
			⭐			
	30 ⭐					

- **Look and write the dates.**

  ⭐ Today is Monday, September 2, 2019.
  ⭐ Today is Friday, September _____.
  ⭐ Today is Wednesday, _____.
  ⭐ Today is _____.

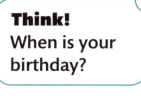

Think! When is your birthday?

Objectives: Identify and write the missing numbers in a calendar. Say the day and date.

- **Listen and say the words.**

classroom

school bus

playground

- **Where are you now? Complete.**

We are in the _____.

Think!
What do you do at the playground?

Unit 1

Objectives: Talk about school activities in different locations at school.

- **Listen and complete the sentence.**

Exploration and Knowing of the World

Learning to Do

Children in Africa like to _____.

Think!
Is your school different from a school in Africa?

- **What do you like to do at school? Draw.**

I like to ...

Objectives: Take care of different locations at school. Talk about likes and dislikes.

● **What do you like to do with your friends at the playground? Draw.**

- **Listen and circle their new friend.**

   Mitzi, Max, and Their New Friend

- **Is their new friend real or imaginary? Complete the sentence.**

   Their new friend is _____.

- **Listen and say the words.**

sun

sand

snake

sad

school

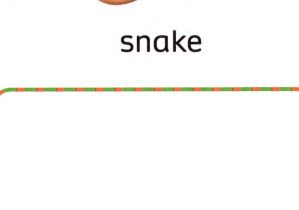

- **Draw a word that begins with the /s/ sound. Write it.**

- **Listen, sing, and clap.**

Unit 1

Objectives: Practice saying words with the /s/ sound.

- **Count and write the number.**

Mathematical Thinking
Learning to Know

 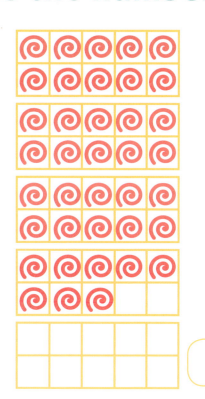 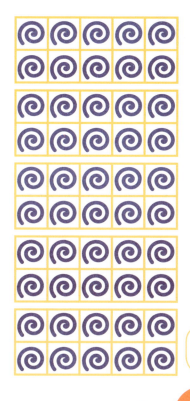

- **Look at the number and draw dots.**

45

Unit 1 25

Objectives: Count to 50. Write numbers to 50.

- **Answer the questions about yourself.**

    What's your name? _____
    How old are you? _____
    Do you like to swim? _____

Language Instruction and Communication
Learning to Know

- **Look and say what happens in the story.**

Objectives: Ask and answer questions about themselves.

- **Listen and match.**

How Do We Learn?

listen

look

understand

do

Think!
What school activity makes you happy?

- **Listen and sing.**

Objectives: Compare personal knowledge.

Unit 1

27

- **Look and color good or wrong.**

- **Read and circle.**

  I'm a good kindergarten citizen.

  Think!
  What kinds of things make you a good kindergarten citizen?

Unit 1

Objectives: Understand the importance of behaving respectfully towards others.

Unit 2 — What parts of your body help you feel?

- Draw the body part you use for each sense.

29

Listen and circle.

David's New Dog

David is sad / happy with his new dog.

Objectives: Listen to and understand a story.

- **Listen and trace.**

Phonemic Awareness
Learning to Know

- **Listen, circle, and trace.**

Diana has a dog.
Dog begins with *d*.
His name is Dinosaur.
He's very big you see!

Objectives: Identify the /d/ sound.

- **Complete the numbers chart.**

- **Follow the color pattern. Color.**

Objectives: Identify and name missing numbers to 50. Extend color pattern.

- **Look, listen, and say.**

Mmm! This honey smells good.

Uh-oh! This cheese smells bad.

- **Circle the correct word.**

smells good / bad

smells good / bad

Objectives: Learn about senses: *smell*.

● **Let's play a game! Cut and paste.**

Find something that ...

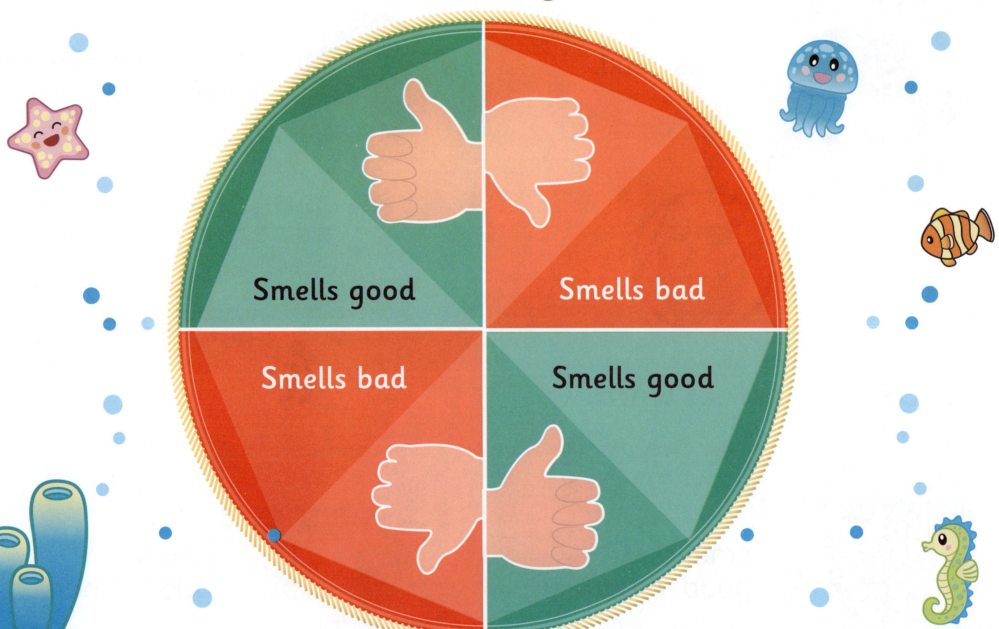

34 Unit 2

Objectives: Recognize food according to their characteristics: *smell*.

● **Look and number the pictures in order.**

Personal, Social, and Emotional Development

Learning to Live Together
Learning to Live with Others

Think!
How many times a day do you wash your hands?

Objectives: Understand how to take care of themselves.

Unit 2

- **Look and complete the title.**

Literacy
Learning to Know

David, Dasher, and the _____

- **Listen and circle the correct answer.**

Which animal is scared?   What does Dasher do?
Dasher / the duck   He runs after the duck. / He runs back to David.

Objectives: Predict the story's name. Answer questions about the story.

- **Look, listen, and say.**

lick　　　　　　　　　look　　　　　　　　lollipop

- **Listen and circle the letter *l*.**

This lollipop looks good!
This lollipop smells sweet!
Let's lick the lollipop
And eat, eat, eat!

Objectives: Identify the /l/ sound.

- **Paste the shapes to complete the patterns.**

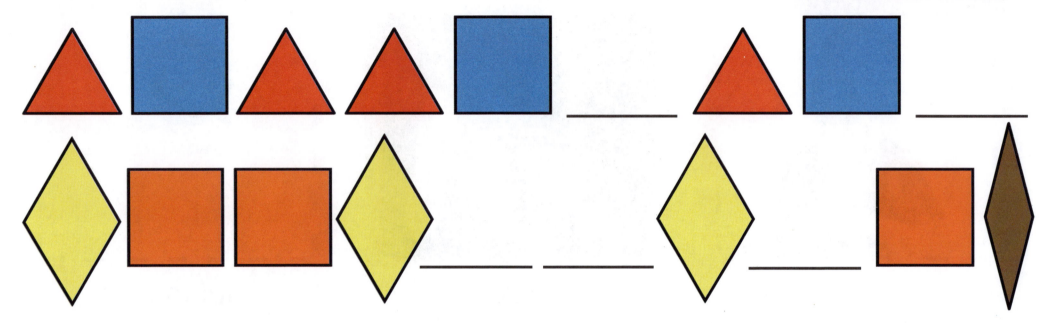

- **Paste shapes to create a pattern.**

Mathematical Thinking
Learning to Know

Objectives: Name shapes. Extend complex patterns.

- **Look, listen, and say.**

It's sweet. It's a donut.   It's sour. It's a lemon.   It's salty. It's a French fry.

- **Draw a picture for each word.**

sweet

sour

salty

Objectives: Describe tastes.

Unit 2

- **Smell and taste the food. Draw.**

Exploration and Knowing of the World
Learning to Do

| smell good | smell bad |
| taste sweet | taste sour |

- **Complete the sentence about your favorite food.**

The _____ smells _____ and tastes _____ .

Unit 2

Objectives: Classify and group food items according to their individual characteristics.

● **Read and draw.**

Personal, Social, and Emotional Development

Learning to Live Together
Learning to Live with Others

| I like to smell… | I like to taste… | I don't like to smell… | I don't like to taste… |

● **Interview a friend and draw.**

My friend…

| likes to smell… | likes to taste… | doesn't like to smell… | doesn't like to taste… |

Think!
Do you respect others' likes and dislikes?

Objectives: Learn how to respect themselves.

Unit 2

- **Look and say. What is the story about?**

Literacy

Learning to Know

David, Dasher, and Lily

- **Listen and circle the correct answer.**

Who is Lily?
She is David's new dog. / She is David's new cat.

Think!
What pet do you like better?

- **Look, listen, and say the words.**

tree   tent   tiger

- **Listen and circle the letter *t*. What is missing in the picture? Say.**

Look at the tent.
It's under a tree.
There's a tiger in the tent,
And it's looking at me!
Help!

- **Cut out and paste. Trace the symmetry lines and color.**

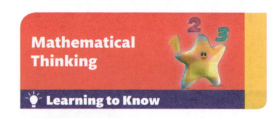
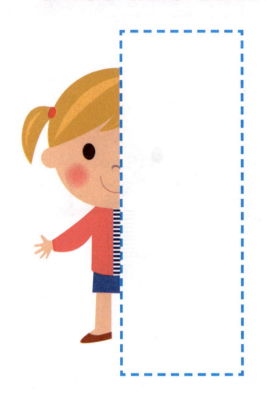
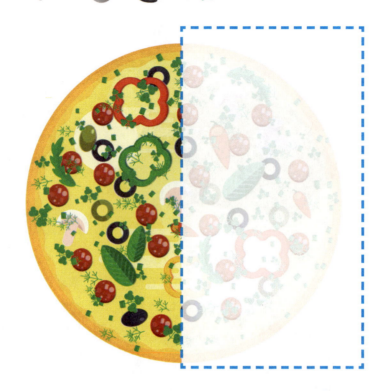

- **Draw the line of symmetry. Color.**

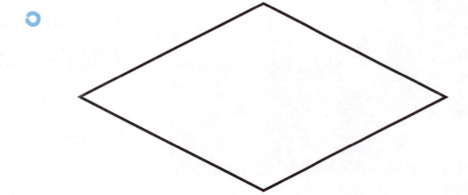

Objectives: Draw a symmetry line.

Listen, point, and say.

drum   triangle   cymbals   tambourine

Listen and circle the correct picture.

It's loud.

It's soft.

Think!
What musical instrument do you like? Is it loud?

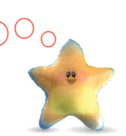

Objectives: Identify and describe *loud* and *soft* sounds.

Unit 2   45

- **Listen to different types of music. Number them in order.** 🎧 ✏️

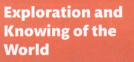

- **Listen and circle the types of music that sound loud.** 🎧 ✏️

Think!
What kind of music do you like to dance?

Unit 2

Objectives: Talk about preferences in music.

- **Listen and match the sentences with the pictures.** 🎧 36

He can draw.

She can read.

Personal, Social, and Emotional Development
♥ Learning to Live Together
Learning to Live with Others

- **What do you have to practice more? Draw a picture in your notebook.** ✏️

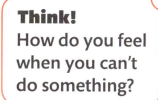

Think!
How do you feel when you can't do something?

Objectives: Learn to face challenges and develop strategies to overcome them.

Unit 2

- **Look and say. Where are they?**

Going Camping

- **Listen and check the correct answer.**

  Who goes camping?
  - ☐ David, Mom, Dad, Dasher, and Lily.
  - ☐ Mom, Dad, Dasher, and Lily.

- **Retell the story.**

Think! What do you like about camping?

Objectives: Retell the story. Give a personal opinion.

- **Match the pictures with their beginning sound. Trace the letters.**

Phonemic Awareness
Learning to Know

- **Trace. Write a name that begins with the /d/ sound.**

Think!
Can you write a name that begins with *L*?

Objectives: Identify the /d/, /l/, /t/ sounds.

Unit 2

- **Color. Use a piece of yarn and measure. Glue it in place.**

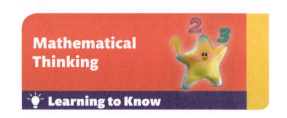

Mathematical Thinking

Learning to Know

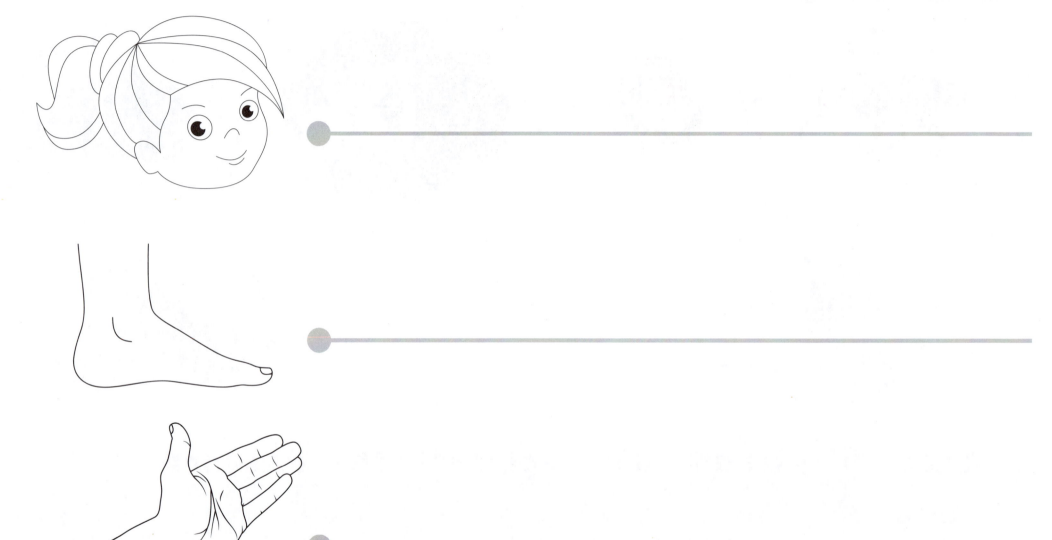

Objectives: Measure and compare body parts using yarn. Begins to use language associated with measurement.

- **Look, listen, point, and say.**

Language Instruction and Communication

Learning to Know

"I don't like these shoes. They're hard."

"I like these slippers. They're soft."

"I don't like this hat. It's rough."

- **Circle the correct word.**

  This sweater is very hard / soft / rough.

- **Draw a hard, soft, and rough object.**

hard	soft	rough

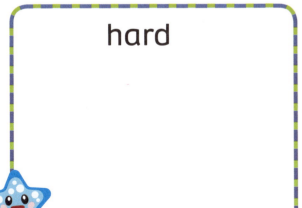

Objectives: Learn about the senses: *touch*. Identify *hard, soft, rough.*

Unit 2

51

- **Listen and say. Do you like spaghetti?**

Exploration and Knowing of the World
Learning to Do

- **Complete the sentence.**

I spaghetti with ____.

Objectives: Identify food they like, and don't like and say why.

- **Listen and say. What's the rule of the game?**

The teacher says, "Hold hands!"

Dance!

- **Cross out the picture that doesn't follow the rule.**

Think! Why is it important to follow the rules of a game?

Objectives: Understand and follow instructions.

Unit 3 Why is your family important to you?

- Draw a happy or a sad face.

My family makes me...

Look, listen, and circle.

Quentin and the New Baby

Quentin has a new brother / sister.

Think!
Is Quentin happy with the new baby?

Objectives: Narrate stories as part of a group. Listen to, understand, and answer questions about a story.

● **Listen and repeat. Trace the letters.**

● **Listen and chant.**

56 Unit 3

Objectives: Identify the /q/ sound.

● **Look and complete the chart.**

● **Trace the numbers.**

2 2 2 2 2 2

4 4 4 4 4 4

6 6 6 6 6 6

- **Match the words to the pictures.**

mom   dad   brother   sister   grandma   grandpa

- **Listen and sing.**

Objectives: Describe family members.

- **Listen and check the things your parents do for you.** 🎧 43 ✔

- **Draw what your parents do for you.** ✏️

Think!
What do you do for your parents?

Objectives: Learn about different family members and their roles.

Unit 3

59

Check where the girl is generous. ✓

Personal, Social, and Emotional Development

Learning to Live Together
Learning to Live with Others

Think!
What do you do in similar situations?

Unit 3

Objectives: Learn to be geneorus, respectful, honest, and tolerant.

- **Listen and trace the baby's name.**

Literacy

Learning to Know

Meeting the New Baby

The baby's name is Zoe.

Think!
What color is Quentin's duckling?

- **Tell the story.**

● **Connect the dots. What letter is it?**

1 2

3 4

● **Listen and repeat.**

Think!
Do you know any other words with the z sound?

● **Listen and sing.**

Objectives: Identify the /z/ sound.

Cut out and paste to continue the patterns. Color.

• **Listen and complete.**

Language Instruction and Communication
Learning to Know

I'm Zack. I'm tall like my dad.

My dad is __tall__.

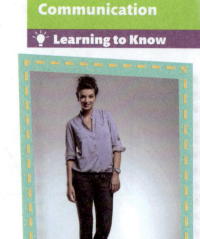

My mom is __thin__.

My sister is __short__.

My baby brother is __young__.

Objectives: Say the differences in people according to: size and age.

● Match the opposites.

Objectives: Talk about responsibilities and chores at home.

Unit 3

65

● **Listen, cut out, and paste.**

Personal, Social, and Emotional Development

Learning to Live Together
Learning to Live with Others

Jane picks up her toys.

Tom helps wash the dishes.

Sheri sets the table.

Millie makes her bed.

● **Draw how you can help at home.**

Unit 3

Objectives: Understand why it is important to be cooperative, respectful, honest, and tolerant.

Look and listen. Circle.

Happy Birthday Quentin!

Listen and circle.

How old is Quentin now? 5 / 6

What is a xylophone? a toy / a musical instrument

Objectives: Listen to, understand, and answer questions about a story.

Unit 3

● **Listen and mark the word that begins with the letter x.** 🎧 X

Phonemic Awareness
Learning to Know

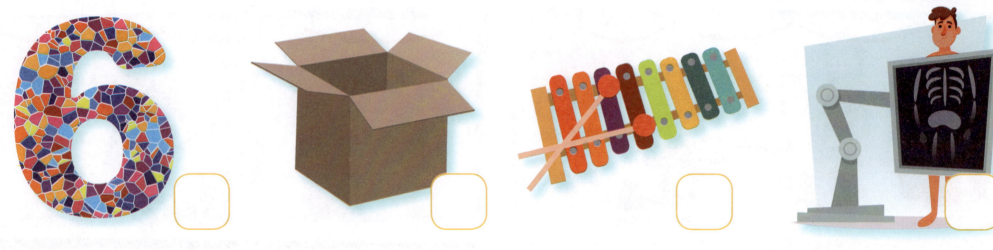

● **Trace the letter x.** ✏️

six
box

xylophone
x-ray

Think!
What are X-rays for?

68 Unit 3

Objectives: Identify the /x/ sound.

● **Count and write the number of people. Color.**

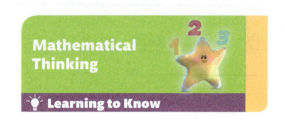

Mathematical Thinking

Learning to Know

- **Listen and check Xavi or Zoila.**

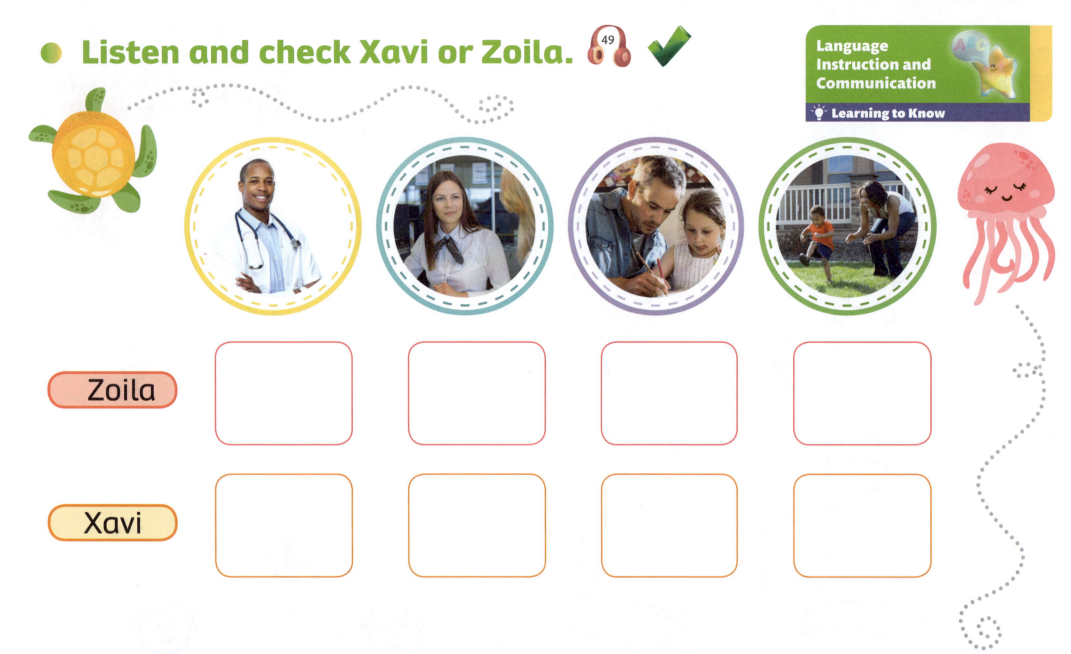

- **Who looks after you? Circle your answer.**

mom   dad   grandma   grandpa   other

70 Unit 3

Objectives: Talk about different kinds of families and their roles.

- **Listen and check the chores you like to do.**

Exploration and Knowing of the World

Learning to Do

I help cook.

I help wash the dog.

I help wash the dishes.

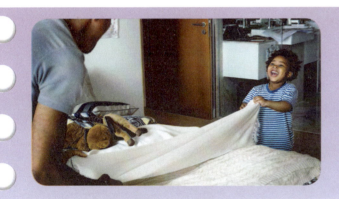

I make my bed.

I put my toys away.

I clean the floor.

Think! Why is doing chores important?

Objectives: Talk about different responsibilities and chores at home.

Unit 3

- **Look and answer.**

Are the children happy or sad?

- **Circle the things you do with your family and friends.**

Objectives: Be enthusiastic when spending time with other boys and girls.

- **Look and answer.**

At the Zoo

Where's Quentin?

How many animals can you see?

- **Listen and tell the story.**

Objectives: Listen to and understand a story. Retell a story.

- **Follow the code and color the xylophone.**

Phonemic Awareness
Learning to Know

Z- brown
z- black
X- gray
x- white
Q- yellow
q- red
D- blue
d- green

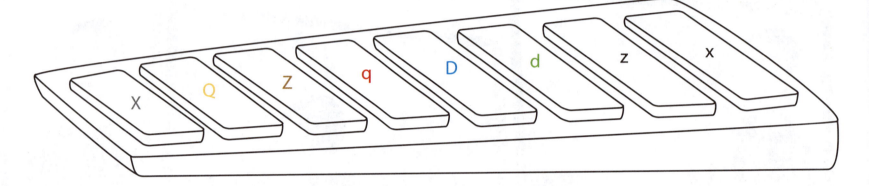

- **Listen and complete.**

___oo   ___uiz   ___ero

si___   bo___   ___ueen

- **Read and circle who weighs more.**

Dad is heavier.   Mom is lighter.   Brother is heavier.   Sister is lighter.

- **Draw something heavier than you.**

● **Listen and put the pictures in order.**

Think!
How many cousins do you have?

● **Answer.**

Who is the girl in the picture? _____

What is her aunt's name? _____

What are her cousins' names? _____

Objectives: Ask and answer questions about family.

● **Say what the children are using. Write the correct word below each picture.**

Exploration and Knowing of the World

Learning to Do

pan   sponge   broom

Think!
What tools do you use at home to do a chore?

Objectives: Identify tools that children can use at home.

Unit 3

● **Check the picture that makes you happy.**

● **Circle the correct answer.**

Playing together is nice / not nice.

Unit 4 What happens to your body when you are hot or cold?

- Color red for hot weather and blue for cold weather.

79

- **Listen and say where Pippa and Paul are.**

Literacy — Learning to Know

Pippa and Paul on Vacation

- **What are Pippa and Paul doing? Circle.**

- **Listen, trace, and match.**

Phonemic Awareness
Learning to Know

pink

purple

purple

pink

- **Listen and clap.**

Objectives: Identify the /p/ sound.

Unit 4

81

- **Count by 2's and write. Extend the color pattern.**

- **Count by 2's. Write the missing numbers.**

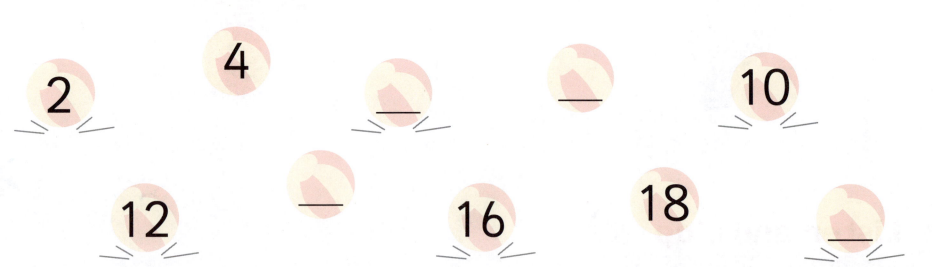

Listen and color.

Objectives: Talk about animals found at the beach.

Unit 4

Think and check the sunny day.

Exploration and Knowing of the World

Learning to Do

Think! What is a shadow?

Unit 4

Objectives: Talk about different kinds of weather.

- **Listen and check the clothes you wear at the beach.**

- **Draw your clothes for the beach. Share.**

Objectives: Express preferences about different types of clothes.

Unit 4

- **Look and say what Pippa and Paul are doing.** 👁 👄

The Sandcastle

- **Listen and check. What are they going to do next?** 🎧 ✔

- ☐ play with sand
- ☐ go swimming

Objectives: Read a story about the beach. Make predictions about a story.

● **Listen and circle the pictures that begin with /p/.**

● **Paste two pictures of words that begin with /p/ sound.**

Objectives: Identify the /p/ sound.

● **Extend the pattern. Cut and paste.**

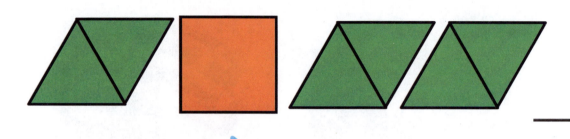

What sea animal is it? Connect the dots.

Language Instruction and Communication

Learning to Know

Think!
What color are sharks?

Objectives: Talk about and describe sea animals.

Unit 4

Listen and put the pictures in order.

Exploration and Knowing of the World
Learning to Do

Unit 4

Objectives: Learn about animals found at the beach.

- **Circle the things you like to do at the beach.**

Personal, Social, and Emotional Development

Learning to Live Together
Learning to Live with Others

Objectives: Talk about activities at the beach and in the water.

Unit 4

● Listen and put the pictures in order.

A Cold Day at the Beach

● Look and circle the weather at the beach.

Objectives: Put the events in sequential order.

- **Listen, say, and trace.**

- **Draw three more words that begin with letter *c*.**

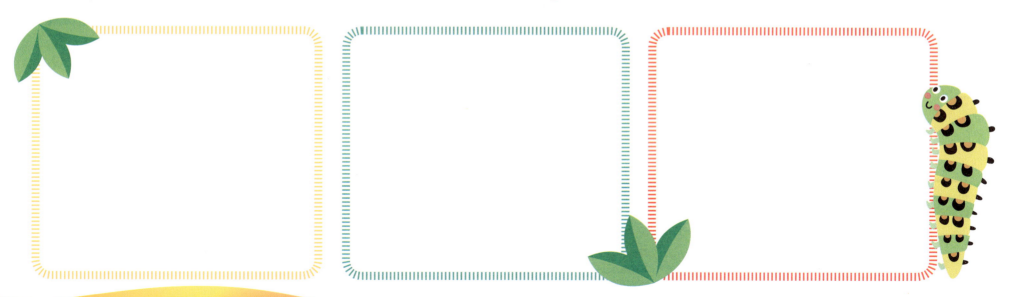

Objectives: Identify a sound of letter *c*.

Paste shapes to create symmetrical patterns.

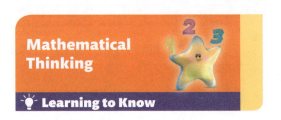

Mathematical Thinking
Learning to Know

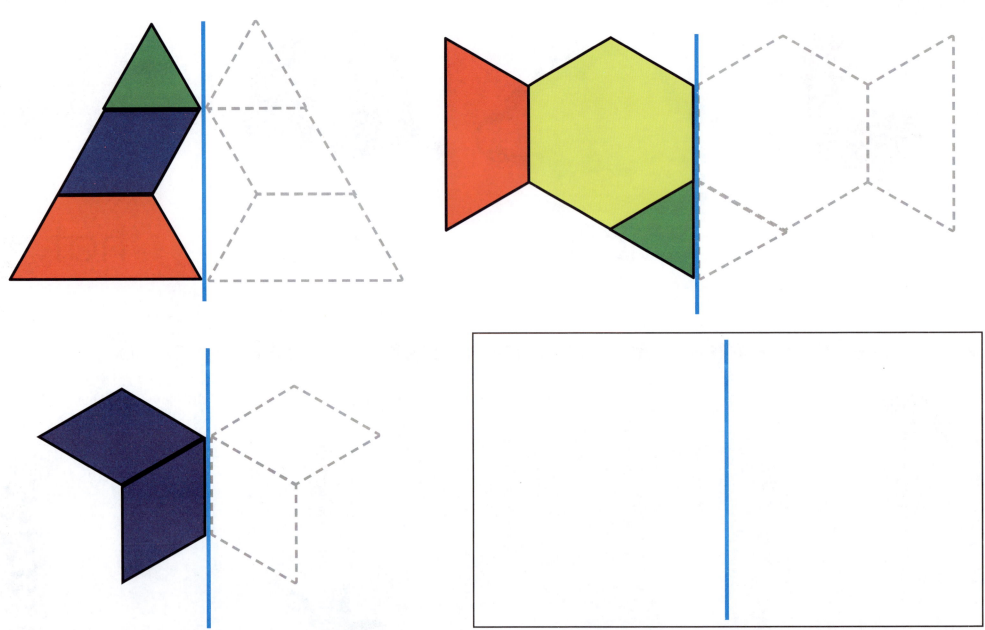

Objectives: Create simple symmetrical patterns.

● **Listen and circle the appropriate clothing.**

Language Instruction and Communication

💡 Learning to Know

Think!
What's the weather like today?

Objectives: Talk about different kinds of weather and clothes.

Unit 4

95

Cut out and paste the pieces of the puzzle.

The Water Cycle

Exploration and Knowing of the World

Learning to Do

Objectives: Learn about a natural process.

Listen and cross out.

Personal, Social, and Emotional Development

Learning to Live Together
Learning to Live with Others

Objectives: Show how to take care of our bodies in different kinds of weather.

Unit 4

Listen and circle the items in the story.

Literacy

Learning to Know

Hello, Dolphins!

Think!
Is a dolphin dangerous?
And a shark?

Unit 4

Objectives: Discuss what is happening in the story.
Make inferences about the story.

- **Listen, trace, and match.**

cloud

crab

cap

cake

- **Listen and chant.**

Think! When do you wear a cap?

Objectives: Identify a sound of letter c.

Unit 4

99

- **Look, think, and circle.**

This is heavier.

This is lighter.

- **Cut out and paste in the correct places.**

| lighter | heavier |

| heavier | lighter |

- **Listen and find the octopus. Circle it.** 🎧63 ✏️

Language Instruction and Communication
Learning to Know

- **Listen and trace.** 🎧64 👄

in on under in front of behind

Objectives: Talk about sea animals. Describe the location of things.

Unit 4

● **Listen and check the correct picture.**

102 Unit 4

Objectives: Talk about living things in different environments.

- **Draw a picture about the beach. Describe it to a friend.** ✏️ 👄

Personal, Social, and Emotional Development

Learning to Live Together
Learning to Live with Others

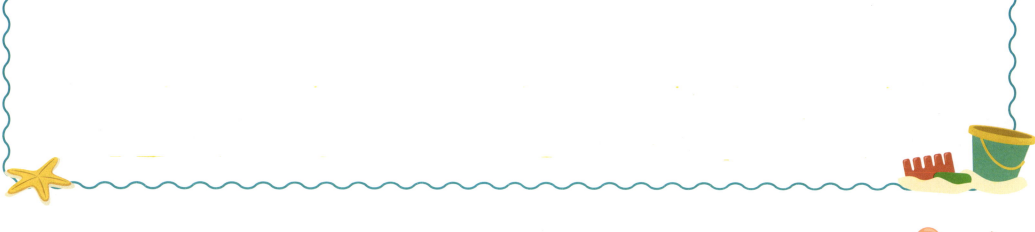

- **Listen to your friend and draw the picture described.** 👂 ✏️

Think! Did you draw similar things?

Objectives: Share experiences with others related to the beach.

Unit 4

- **Is the sun shining today? Look and say.**

Rain, Rain Go Away!

- **Listen and circle.**

Do Pippa and Paul want to have lunch? Yes / No

- **Finger paint the letters.**

B b

- **Listen and complete the words.**

_acon   _each   _illy

- **Count and write the number of sea animals. Color.**

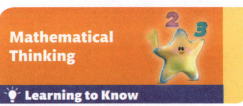

Mathematical Thinking
Learning to Know

● **Complete the pictures. Match.**

It is windy.   It is rainy.

Objectives: Talk about weather and clothes.

● **Listen and choose the correct answer.**

Exploration and Knowing of the World
Learning to Do

Dolphins are fish / mammals.

108 Unit 4

Objectives: Notice similarities and differences between people and animals..

Put the pictures in order.

Personal, Social, and Emotional Development

Learning to Live Together
Learning to Live with Others

Objectives: Learn about getting dressed for the weather.

Unit 4

109

- **Is this the end of the vacation? Look and say.**

Good-bye, Vacation!

- **Listen and circle who the children say good-bye to. Tell the story.**

Unit 4

Objectives: Retell a story.

● **Connect the dots. Listen and repeat.**

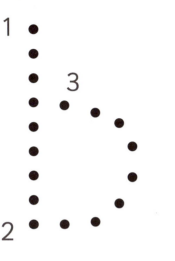 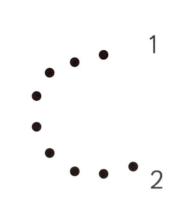 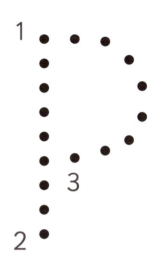

● **Listen, say, and match.**

The cake is on the plate.

The crab is in the pail.

The cookies are in the picnic basket.

Objectives: Identify the sound of letters *b*, *p*, and *c*.

● **Count the sea animals and draw a dot for each one. Write the number.**

Mathematical Thinking
Learning to Know

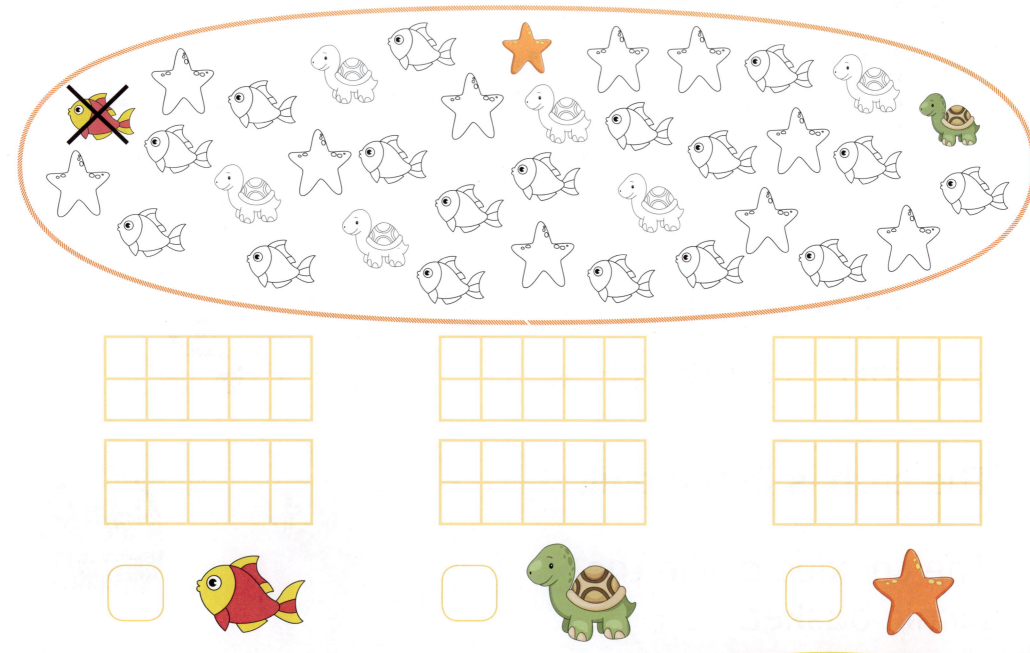

- **Match the animals to the place where you can find them.**

Language Instruction and Communication
Learning to Know

Objectives: Talk about sea animals.

● **Listen and check or cross out.** 🎧

☐ Starfish live on the beach.

☐ Starfish eat fish.

☐ Starfish live for 10 years.

- **Choose and color a type of weather. Draw a picture of yourself in that weather.**

Personal, Social, and Emotional Development

Learning to Live Together
Learning to Live with Others

Objectives: Share experiences with others relating to weather.

Unit 4

Unit 5 Why is it important to take care of our planet?

- What are the children doing? Complete.

They are _____.

- **Listen. Color the main characters.**

No, Neddy!

- **Color and say.**

- **Listen and circle the letter *n*.**

No, Neddy!
It's nine.
Time to go to bed.
No, Neddy!
It's nine.
Time for bed, I said.

Objectives: Identify the /n/ sound.

- **Count by 2's and write the missing numbers. Extend the color pattern.**

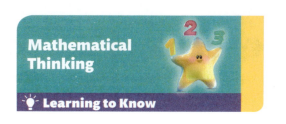

Mathematical Thinking

Learning to Know

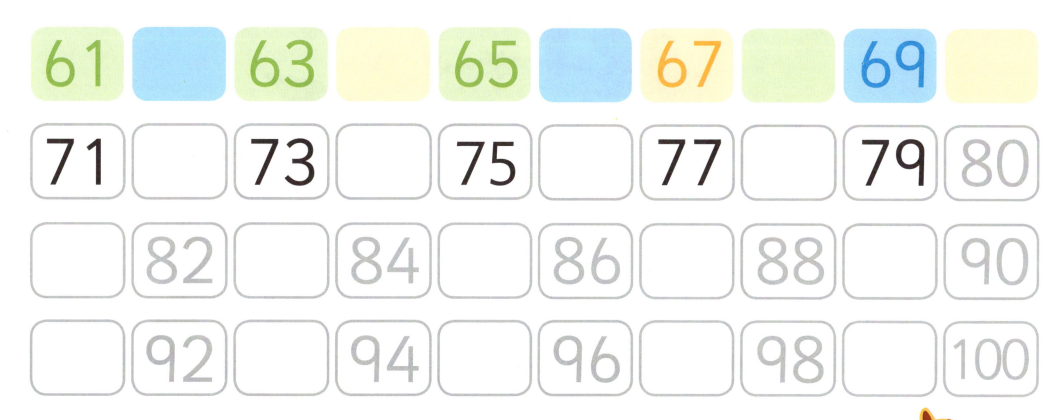

- **Write the numbers that come before and after.**

| | 63 | | | | 75 | | | | 86 | |

● Look and circle.

We share / don't share the planet.

- **Circle what you can find in your garden.**

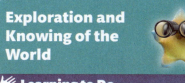

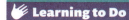

- **Draw two living things in each box.**

 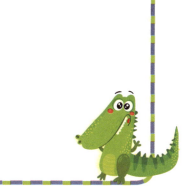

Plants and animals that live in the garden.

Plants and animals that don't live in the garden.

Objectives: Learn where you can find different plants and animals.

Unit 5

121

● **Can you guess the animal in danger? Cut and paste.**

Personal, Social, and Emotional Development
Learning to Live Together
Learning to Live with Others

122 Unit 5

Objectives: Identify endangered animals. Talk about how they can be helped.

Listen and check the correct option.

Neddy's Flowers

Neddy learned to...

◯ save water ◯ draw flowers

- **Connect the dots and say the letters' sound.**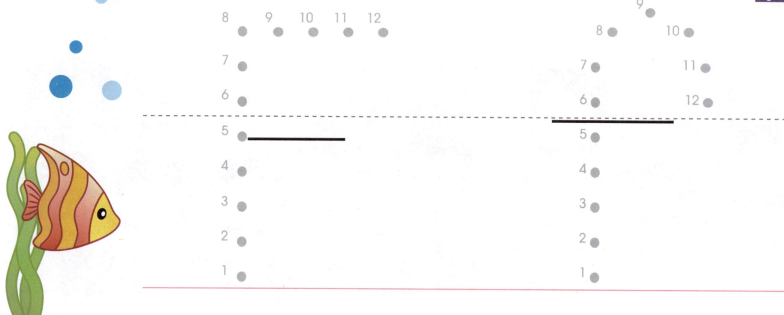

Phonemic Awareness
Learning to Know

- **Listen and complete.**

___lamingo

___laps

___lying!

Unit 5

Objectives: Identify the /f/ sound.

Complete the patterns.

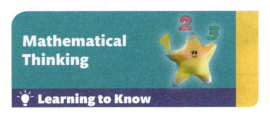

Mathematical Thinking

Learning to Know

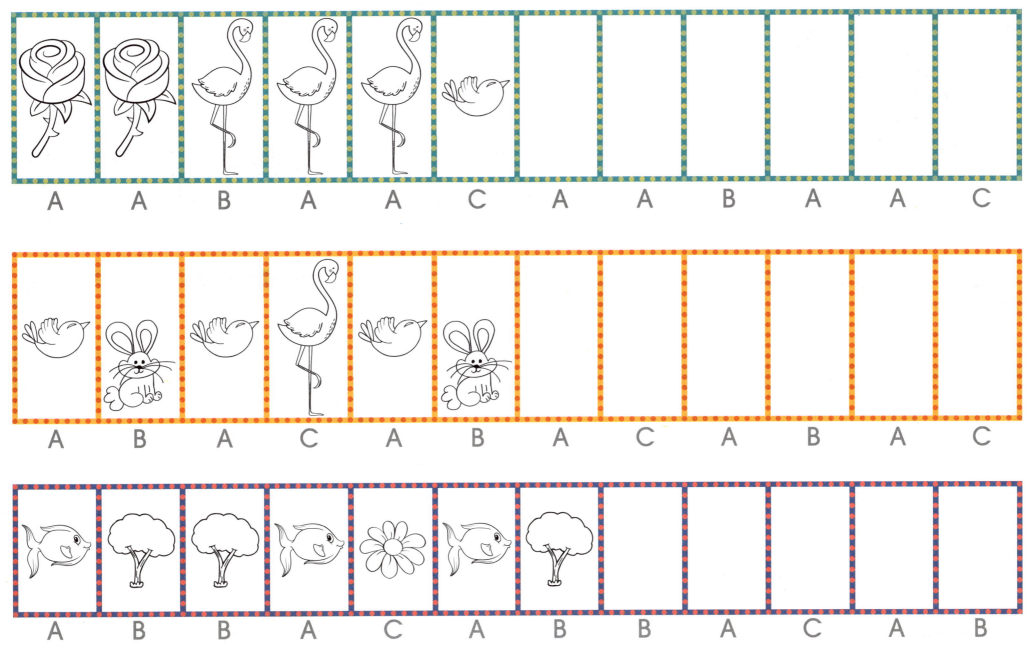

Unit 5

• Trace. Listen and draw.

desert   Arctic   jungle

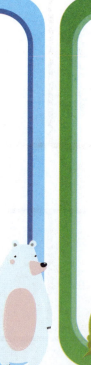
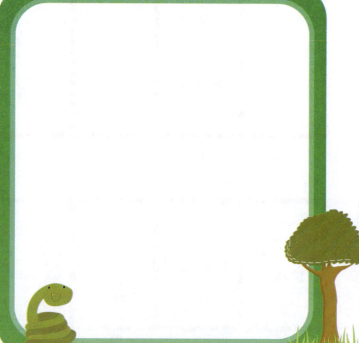

Objectives: Name the different habitats for animals and plants.

- **Listen and match.**

Don't use plastic bottles.

Don't waste paper.

- **Choose a problem. Draw a picture on how to solve it.**

- **Draw the things that make you happy at a park.**

- **Circle and complete.**

A clean / dirty park makes me ◯.

- **Look and describe the pictures. Circle who needs help.**

The Rabbit in the Trap

- **Listen and complete.**

_____ learns to look after animals.

Objectives: Describe pictures in a story. Generate new ideas about a story.

- **Listen and repeat.**

Phonemic Awareness
Learning to Know

- **Read and trace.**

Look at the rabbit.

The rose is  red.

The  and the  are by the .

130 Unit 5

Objectives: Identify the /r/ sound.

- Cut out and paste.

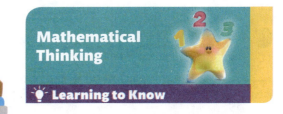

Mathematical Thinking
Learning to Know

Natural Objects

Man-made Objects

Objectives: Sort objects according to their nature.

Unit 5

131

- **Listen and match.**

Objectives: Talk about how to take care of the environment (dos and don'ts).

Look and complete.

Saving _____

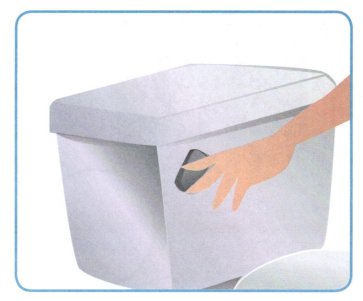

Objectives: Learn how to save water. Understand that the planet is ours and we share it with others.

How do the pictures make you feel? Draw.

Personal, Social, and Emotional Development

Learning to Live Together
Learning to Live with Others

Unit 5

Objectives: Express how problems in the environment make them feel.

Listen and check the answer.

Neddy's Dirty Hands

What will Neddy do before eating a brownie?
☐ wash his face   ☐ wash his hands

- **Complete the words.**

__f__ish   __r__abbit   __n__est

- **Listen, say, and clap.**

Flash the is very funny.

Robbie the likes .

It's .

Natty is asleep in her .

Unit 5

Objectives: Identify the /f/, /r/, and /n/ sounds.

Think, cut, and paste.

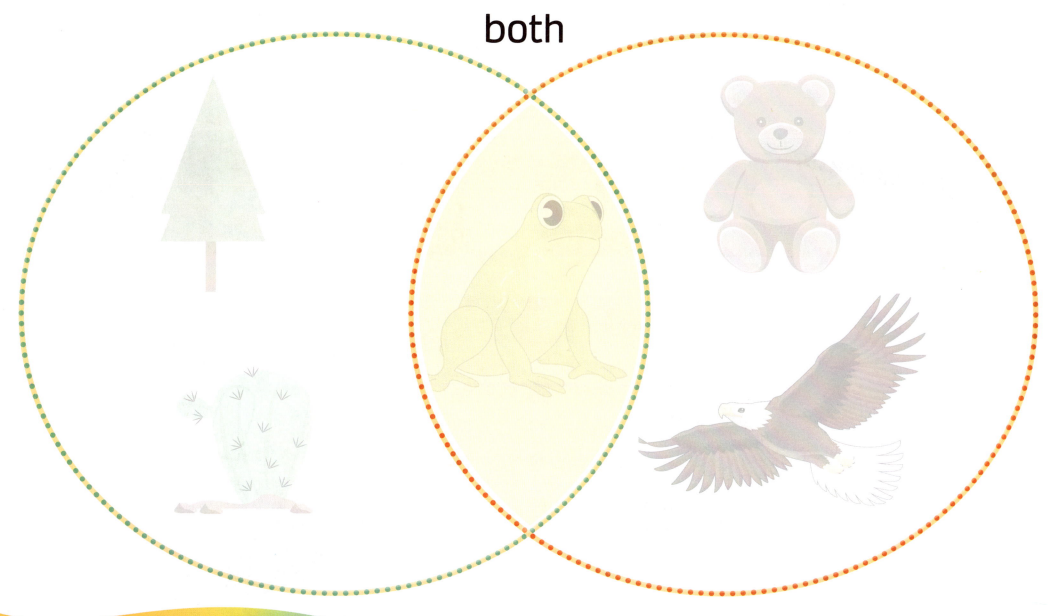

Listen and number the pictures in order.

Let's make a Bird Feeder!

- # Think and match.

Think!
How can you reuse a shoebox?

Objectives: Talk about how to recycle and reuse everyday items.

- What causes these problems? Circle.

Personal, Social, and Emotional Development

Learning to Live Together
Learning to Live with Others

- What can you do to reduce air pollution? Draw.

Unit 5

Objectives: Talk about how to help the environment.

Unit 6 How can you stay healthy?

- Are they happy? Look and say.

● **Look and listen. Put the pictures in order.**

Gordon and the Whizzer

Think!
Who gets to the river first? Why?

● **Retell the story.**

Unit 6

Objectives: Listen to, understand, answer questions about a story. Retell a story.

- **Trace, listen, and complete.**

uitar

arden

Gg

irl

orilla

- **Listen, chant, and do.**

Objectives: Identify the /g/ sound.

- **Draw balls in the ten frames. Add and write.**

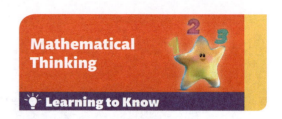
Mathematical Thinking — Learning to Know

 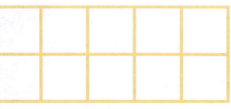  

10 + 3 = 13   10 + 6 = ___   10 + 2 = ___   10 + 8 = ___

10 + 9 = ___   10 + 4 = ___   10 + 1 = ___   10 + 10 = ___

Objectives: Use the double ten frame to add numbers.

● **Check the things you do. Cross out the things you don't do.** ✔ ✘

● **Tell the class about your healthy habits.**

I eat vegetables.

I go to bed early.

Think!
How can you stay healthy?

Objectives: Learn key words for healthy habits.

Unit 6 — **145**

● **Listen and circle the correct answer.**

Exploration and Knowing of the World
Learning to Do

Stomachache

Drink some tea / milk.

Sore throat

Have some water / honey.

Cold

Go to the park / bed.

Fever

Call the teacher / doctor.

146 Unit 6

Objectives: Provide verbal solutions to health problems.

- **Listen, describe, and check.**

Who helps Charlie?
- ☐ the girl
- ☐ the teacher

Objectives: Find out who needs help and how to help them.

Listen and circle the part of the story that is a fantasy.

Literacy

Learning to Know

Down the Rainbow

Objectives: Distinguish fantasy from reality in a reading text.

- **Listen and circle the beginning letter.**

heart　　　　　　　hat　　　　　　　house

- **Listen, sing, and do.**

Objectives: Identify the /h/ sound.

Measure, cut, and paste yarn.

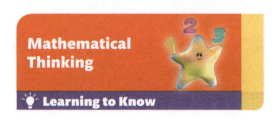

My 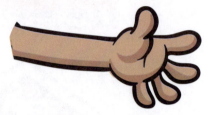 measures this long.

My  measures this long.

My 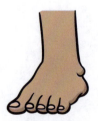 measures this long.

Objectives: Measure body parts using yarn.

Cut out, read, and paste.

I stay healthy when I ...

swim

run

hop

jump

Objectives: Learn key words for healthy habits.

Check the healthy actions.
Cross out the unhealthy actions. ✔ ✘

Exploration and Knowing of the World

Learning to Do

Unit 6

Objectives: Talk about staying healthy.

- **Cut and paste.**

Happy

Sad

Objectives: Talk about feelings.

Listen and draw Jumbo.

The Big Ball

Objectives: Describe pictures in the story.

- **Listen and circle the odd word out.**

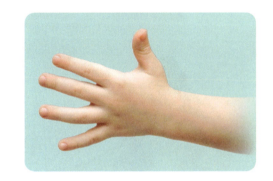

- **Trace and draw.**

Objectives: Identify the /g/ and /h/ sounds.

Unit 6

- **Think and draw a line from the foods to the correct side of the circle.**

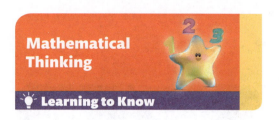

Mathematical Thinking

Learning to Know

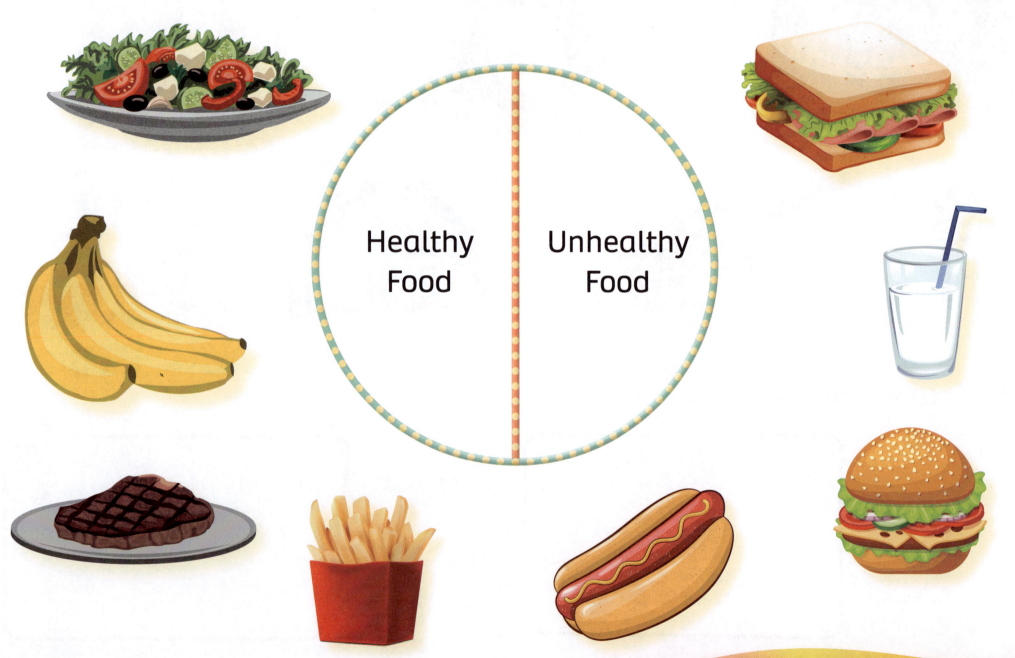

Healthy Food | Unhealthy Food

Objectives: Begins to sort objects using two attributes.

Listen and point. Draw how they feel.

What's the problem?

I have a cold.

I have a cough.

I have a headache.

I have a toothache.

Objectives: Use words related to feelings when they feel well or ill.

Unit 6

- **Check the food you like to eat.**

- **Draw your favorite vegetable.**

Think!
Do you know the name of your favorite vegetable?

Unit 6

Objectives: Understand that some foods promote good health. Name fruits and vegetables.

Draw and complete.

Personal, Social, and Emotional Development
Learning to Live Together
Learning to Live with Others

Healthy food I like.

Healthy food I don't like.

Eating healthy food is _____ for me.

Eating unhealthy food is _____ for me.

Objectives: Express likes and dislikes.

Unit 6

- **Listen and circle the flying kite.**

The Kitten and the Kite

- **Color your favorite character.**

Objectives: Say who their favorite character is in the story.

● **Listen and chant. Trace.**

kite

kitten

kangaroo

kiss

Objectives: Identify the /k/ sound.

Unit 6

● **Complete the symmetrical figures.**

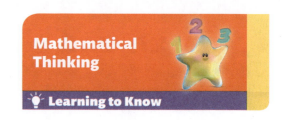

162 Unit 6

Objectives: Complete symmetrical figures.

- Listen and match.

Language Instruction and Communication

Learning to Know

Think!
How many times a day do you brush your teeth?

Objectives: Describe health problems.

Unit 6

Look, think, and say.

 **Is sugar bad for your teeth?**

Imagine these cups are your teeth.

Put two spoons of yeast in the cups.

Put warm water in the cups.

Put sugar in one cup.

Stir!

Look at the second cup. That's sugar on your teeth!

Objectives: Understand that some food and drinks do not promote good health.

- **Circle.**

  I like / don't like snacks.

- **Draw two healthy snacks.**

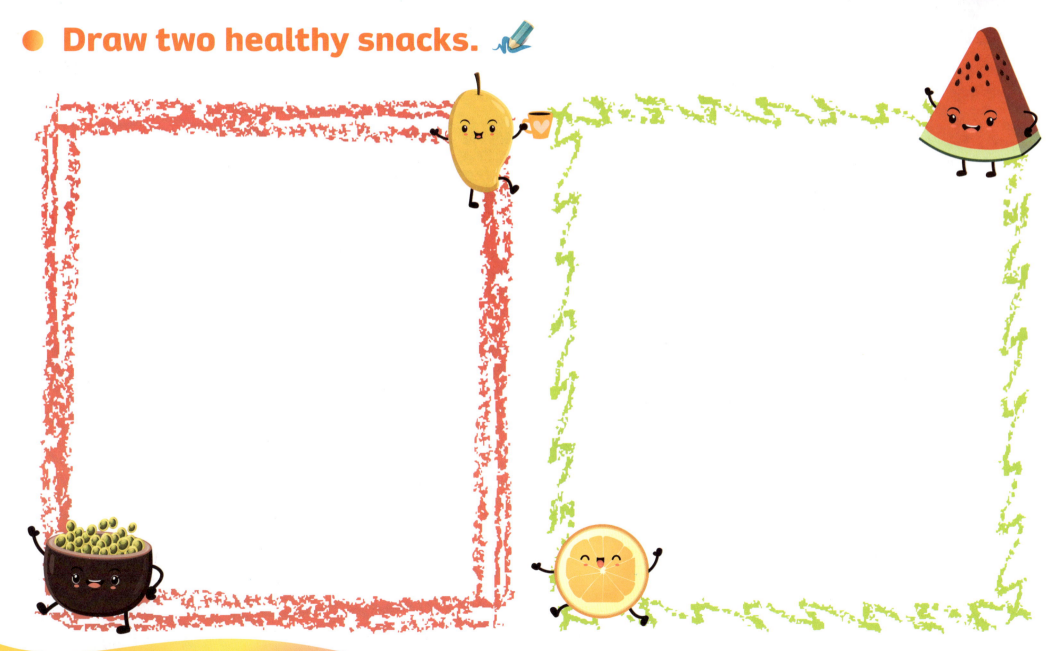

Objectives: Express likes and dislikes.

Listen and complete the scenes.

Jogging with Jenny

Literacy

Learning to Know

Objectives: Describe pictures in the story.

- Color the letters.

J j

- Listen and say the words.

Objectives: Identify the /j/ sound.

Unit 6

Complete the patterns.

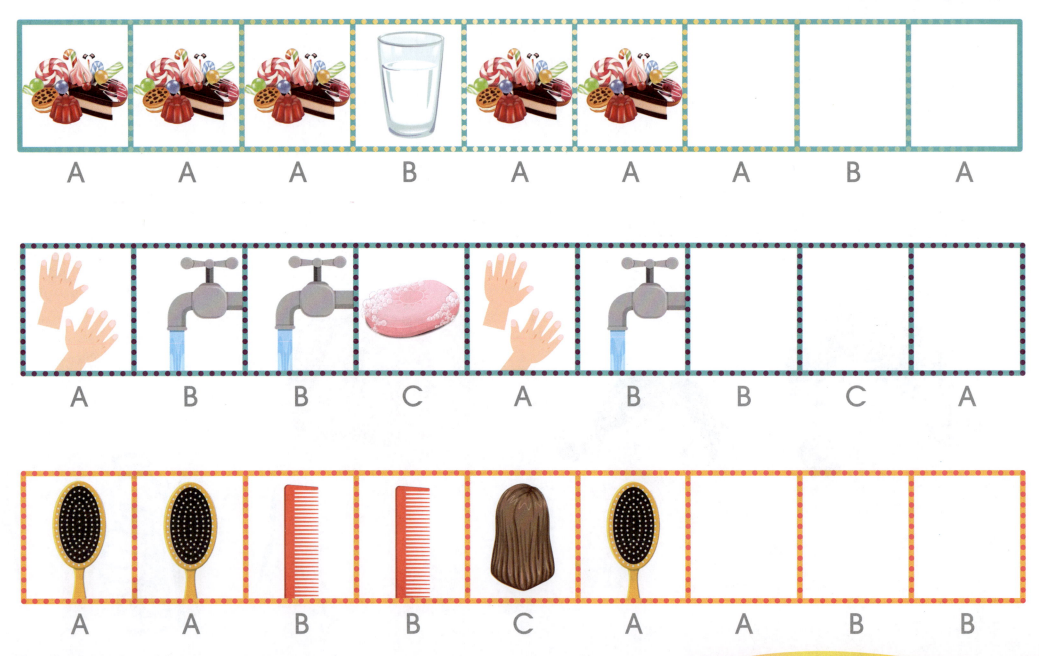

Put the pictures in order.

Language Instruction and Communication
Learning to Know

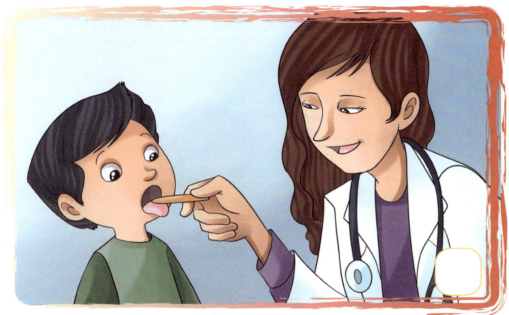

Objectives: Use words related to feelings when they feel ill. Talk about and describe health problems.

Unit 6

- **Cross out the dangerous situations.** ✗

170 Unit 6

Objectives: Learn how to be safe at home.

- **Look, think, and draw what happens next.**

Personal, Social, and Emotional Development

Learning to Live Together
Learning to Live with Others

Don't leave your toys on the floor!

- **Circle the correct word.**

Toys on the floor are safe / dangerous.

Think!
Why is it dangerous to leave objects on the floor?

Objectives: Learn how to be safe at home. Share personal experiences.

- **Look and circle the objects in the story.**

Gordon and the Whizzer to the Rescue

- **Listen and circle.**

Gordon rescues the carrots / dog.

- **Look and say the words.**

- **Trace the letters and draw two pictures.**

Objectives: Identify words that begin with letters *k* and *j*.

Unit 6 — 173

● **Find the objects in the picture and circle them.**

Mathematical Thinking
Learning to Know

● **Read and circle.**

The boy is behind / in front of the mirror.
The towel is to the left / right of the boy.
The toothbrushes are to the left / right of the boy.

Objectives: Talk about the location of things.

- **How are the children feeling? Draw.**

- **Draw.**

I feel happy when I...

Choose healthy food for lunch. Color.

It's Lunch Time!

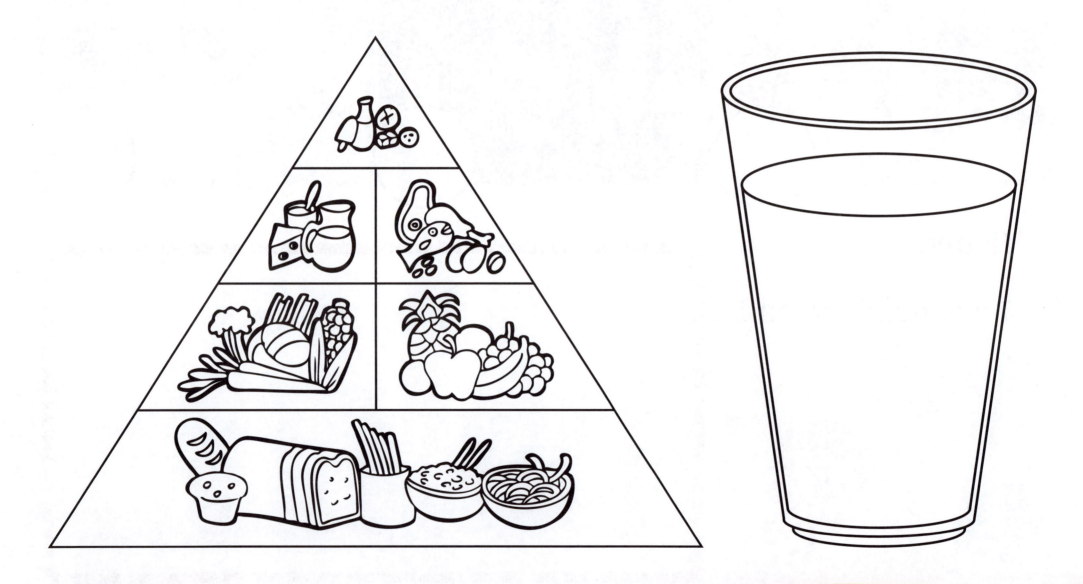

Objectives: Understand that some food and drinks promote good health. Name food and drinks.

Follow the steps.

Let's Go Fishing!

Personal, Social, and Emotional Development

Learning to Live Together
Learning to Live with Others

Think!
Do you like the food you fished?

Objectives: Express likes and dislikes.

Unit 6

Unit 7 How can you take care of animals?

- What is the boy doing? Look and say.

Listen and complete.

Peter and the Wolf (Part I)

Literacy
Learning to Know

Peter lives in the _____.

Objectives: Listen to, understand, answer questions about a story. Retell a story.

Unit 7

● Color.

W w

Phonemic Awareness
Learning to Know

● Listen and complete.

 ___olf

 ___oods

 ___ater

 ___indow

- **Complete the ten frames and write the missing numbers.**

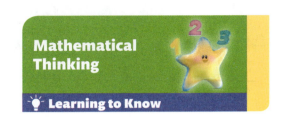

Mathematical Thinking
Learning to Know

8 + __ = 10   6 + __ = 10   1 + __ = 10

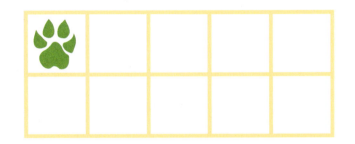

2 + __ = 10   4 + __ = 10   9 + __ = 10

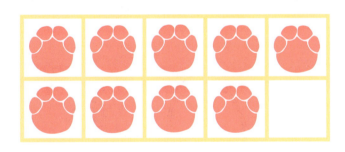

Objectives: Use a ten frame to add numbers to 10.

Unit 7

- **Color the wild animals.**

Language Instruction and Communication

Learning to Know

giraffe

tiger

penguins

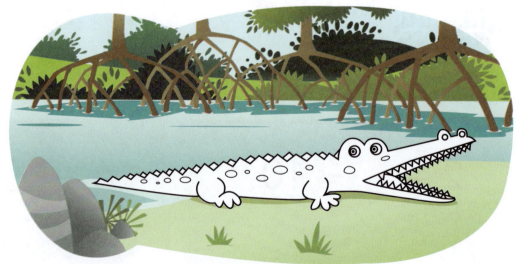

crocodile

Objectives: Learn words for wild animals.

- **Cut out and paste.**

Exploration and Knowing of the World

Learning to Do

fur feathers scales

Objectives: Classify animals. Talk about characteristics of animals.

Unit 7

- **How can you learn to respect animals? Look, say, and draw one more way.**

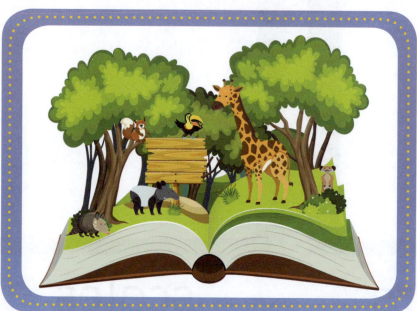

Objectives: Learn to behave respectfully towards animals.

● **Listen and circle the picture where Peter is scared. Say why.**

Peter and the Wolf (Part II)

● Listen and say. Complete.

Phonemic Awareness
Learning to Know

_v_ olcano

_v_ la _v_ a

_v_ iolin

_v_ est

_v_ ase

_v_ an

● Listen and chant.

186

Objectives: Identify the /v/ sound.

Count the animals and color in the graph.

Mathematical Thinking

Learning to Know

Objectives: Make a simple graph to show the number of items.

Unit 7

187

- **Match.**

- **Listen and point.**

Think!
Can you describe a hippo?

188 Unit 7

Objectives: Describe animals and their physical characteristics.

- **Listen and put the pictures in order.**

Objectives: Describe and talk about living things.

- **Work in pairs. Draw, cut, and paste animals.**

- **Circle.**

It's fun / It isn't fun working with my friends.

- **Look at the pictures and tell the story.**

Literacy
Learning to Know

Peter and the Wolf (Part III)

- **Listen and circle the correct sentence.**

The  catches .    catches the .

Objectives: Listen to a story. Answer questions, retell the story and discuss what happened.

Unit 7

- **Trace and match. Listen and say.**

Phonemic Awareness
Learning to Know

yarn   yak   yacht   yellow

Objectives: Identify the /y/ sound.

- **Complete the patterns.**

Mathematical Thinking

Learning to Know

- **Draw a toy on the bottom.**

- **Count and say. How many toys are at the top?**

- **Check the animals that you are afraid of.**

- **Complete and draw.**

My friend is scared of _____.

- **Put the pictures in order.**

Peter and the Wolf (Part IV)

- **Listen and check your answers.**

Objectives: Put parts of a story in sequential order. Make predictions about a story.

● Look and say.

Phonemic Awareness
Learning to Know

volcano

yak

violin

wolf

window

yacht

● Write the words in the boxes.

| w | v | y |

- **What time is it? Write.**

  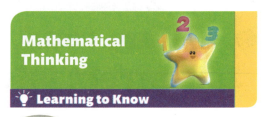 

:00   :00   :00

- **Look and draw the blue hour hand.**

6:00   11:00   9:00

Objectives: Read the time on the hour.

Listen, read, and cross out the incorrect information. 🎧 ❌

Language Instruction and Communication
💡 Learning to Know

Cheetahs

Cheetahs have spots and long tails.

Cheetahs' babies are cubs.

Cheetahs eat plants. They are carnivorous.

Cheetahs live in the sea in Africa.

Objectives: Describe animals and their physical characteristics. Understand new vocabulary words in context.

Look and circle. Cross out what's not the animal's home.

Exploration and Knowing of the World

Learning to Do

wild / domestic

wild / domestic

wild / domestic

Objectives: Understand that animals are part of the natural environment. Learn how to take care of and protect animals.

● **Circle the things you need to live.**

● **Draw two things wildlife needs to live.**

Objectivesw: Be cooperative, tolerant, honest and behave respectfully towards others.

Unit 8 Which is your favorite place in town?

- **Where are the children? Circle.**

They are at the park / in the classroom.

- **Listen and check. Do Miranda and Mike like their new town?**

New in Town

☐ yes   ☐ no

204   Unit 8

Objectives: Listen to, understand, and answer questions about a story.

● **Listen and say. Complete.**

_____useum

_____ovie theater

_____arket

● **Draw pictures of two words that begin with *m*.**

Objectives: Practice the /m/ sound.

Unit 8　**205**

Count, color, and solve the additions.

9 + 5 = __

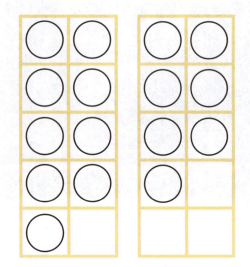

__ + __ = __

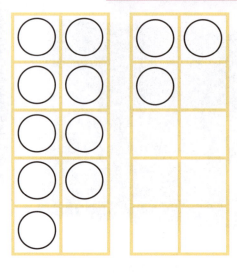

__ + __ = __

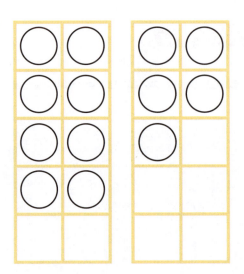

__ + __ = __

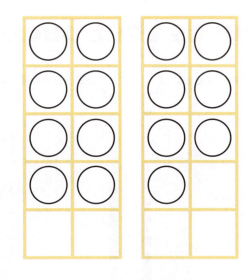

__ + __ = __

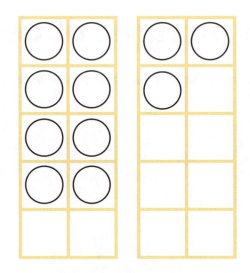

__ + __ = __

Mathematical Thinking
Learning to Know

Objectives: Solve simple additions.

● **Listen and match.**

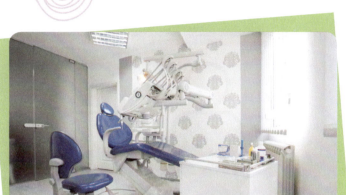

street cleaner

baker

dentist

Objectives: Learn the words for community workers and places in town.

● **Color the signs you know. Draw a different one.**

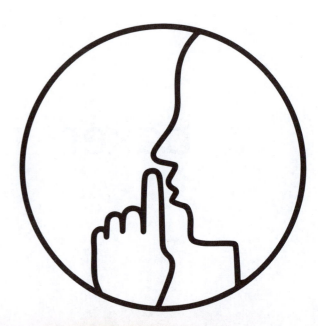

● **Look, listen, and complete.**

Men and _____ work at the health clinic.

Objectives: Understand that boys and girls can do the same activities.

- **Look and say. How many places do Miranda and Mike go to today?** 👁️ 👄

New Shoes

- **Listen and color Mike's new shoes.**

- **Listen and say. Trace.**

street

supermarket

stall

sign

Think!
How do you move around town?

- **Listen, sing, and do.**

Objectives: Identify the /s/ sound.

Unit 8

Look, count, and color the graph.

Mathematical Thinking

Learning to Know

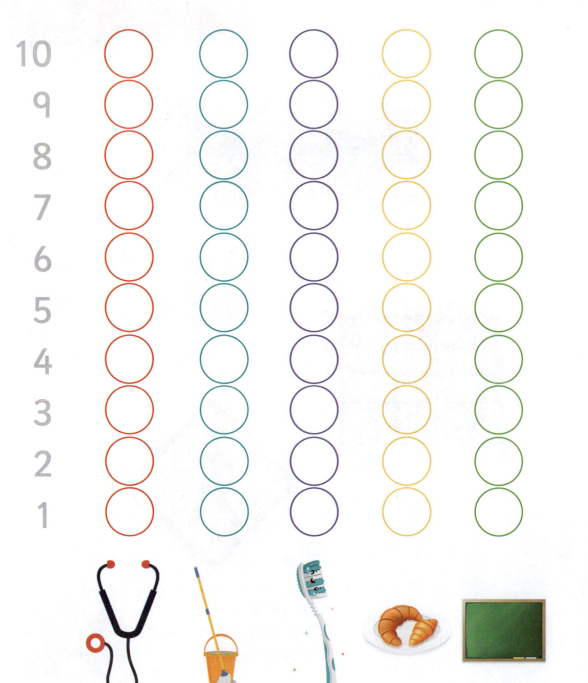

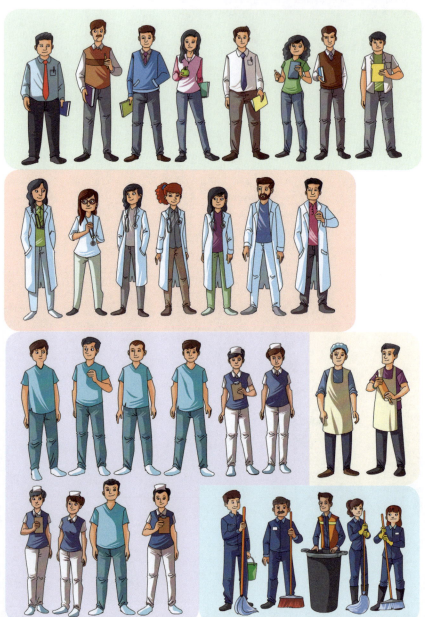

● **Listen and circle the correct picture.**

Firefighters work at the fire station.

Firefighters get on the fire truck.

Firefighters put out fires.

Objectives: Use complete sentences to describe the community workers' actvities.

● **Trace and match.**

friends

teachers

family

● **Draw yourself with your friends.**

214 Unit 8

Objectives: Acknowledge that they are all part of different groups of people: family, school, friends, and community.

● **Listen and point. Circle the correct option.** 🦻 ✏️

    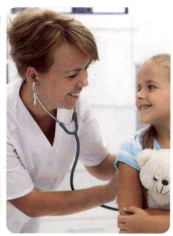 

She is
the nurse / janitor.

She is
the teacher / principal.

He is
the janitor / Stan.

Objectives: Understand that people are different, and everyone's participation is important.

- **Look and complete the title of the story.**

At the _____

- **Listen and check your answer.**

Unit 8

Objectives: Make predictions about the story.

- **Color the letters and match.**

- **Listen and chant.**

Objectives: Identify the /l/ and /d/ sounds.

Unit 8 **217**

- **Write the time.**

:00   :00   :00

- **Read and draw the clock hands.**

It's 5 o'clock.   It's 1 o'clock.   It's 10 o'clock.

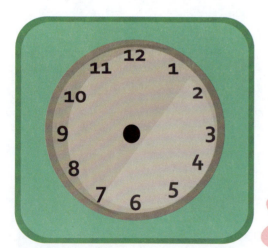  

Objectives: Read the time on the hour.

● **Listen and put the pictures in the correct order.** 👂 ✏️

Language Instruction and Communication
Learning to Know

Objectives: Learn key words for workplace activities and tools.

Unit 8

● **Look at the pictures and guess the place. Complete.**

Exploration and Knowing of the World

Learning to Do

It's a... _____.

It's a... _____.

It's a... _____.

220 Unit 8

Objectives: Identify different public places in their community.

- **Draw three people that work at the place in the picture.**

- **Circle the most important job at the restaurant.**

Objectives: Understand that people are different and everyone's participation is important.

Unit 8   **221**

- **Look and say what happens in each picture.**

New Town, New School

- **Listen and complete.**

Miranda and Mike are _____ in their new school.

Objectives: Discuss what is happening in the story.

- **Listen and say the numbers.** 🎧 👄

    2 ⌒ 10 ⌒ 12 ⌒ 20

- **Draw two words with the /t/ sound.** ✏️

Phonemic Awareness
Learning to Know

Objectives: Identify the /t/ sound.

Unit 8

- Draw.

Mathematical Thinking

Learning to Know

In math class I like to…

In math class I like to…

224 Unit 8

Objectives: Represent and talk about their favorite math activities.

● **Match the community workers with their tools.**

Objectives: Recall key words for workplaces, workplace activities and community workers.

Unit 8

225

- **Cut and paste. Match the worker to the work place.**

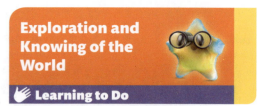

Exploration and Knowing of the World

Learning to Do

Unit 8

Objectives: Identify community workers in their neighborhood and understand what they do.

- **Look and say what the children are doing in the classroom.**

- **Circle the things you can do at school to keep it clean.**

Objectives: Help out in the classroom and at school.

Unit 8

Unit 2, page 44

Unit 3, page 66

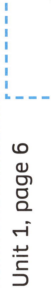
Unit 1, page 6

229

Unit 5, page 137

Unit 4, page 96

231

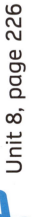

Unit 7, page 183

Unit 8, page 226

Unit 6, page 151

233

Mathematical Thinking, Pattern Blocks

Mathematical Thinking, Pattern Blocks

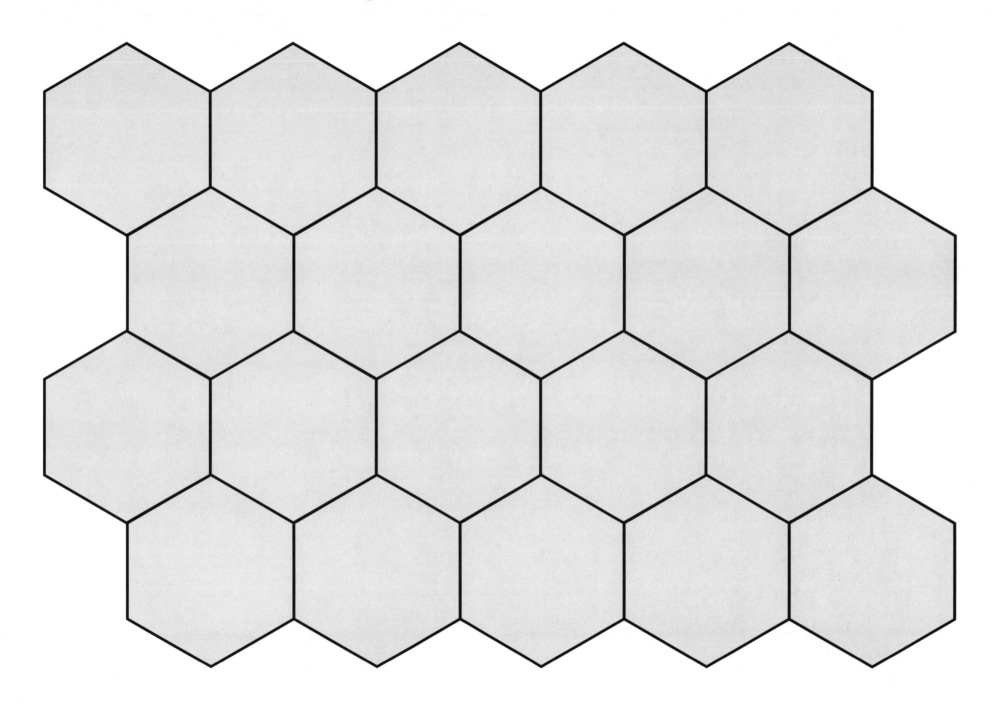

Mathematical Thinking, Pattern Blocks

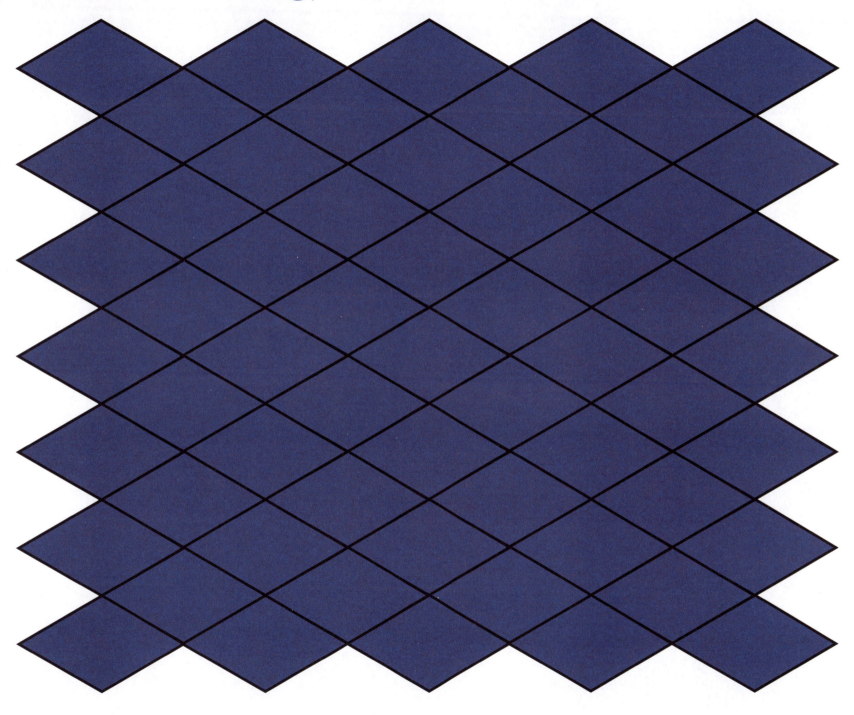

239

Mathematical Thinking, Pattern Blocks

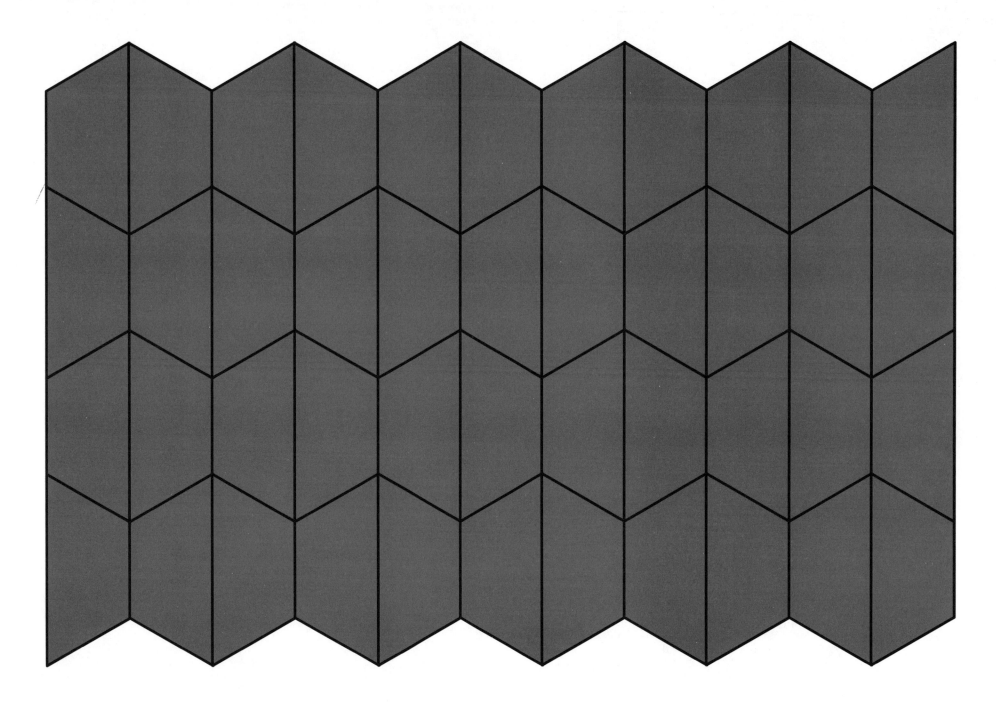

Mathematical Thinking, Pattern Blocks

Mathematical Thinking, Pattern Blocks

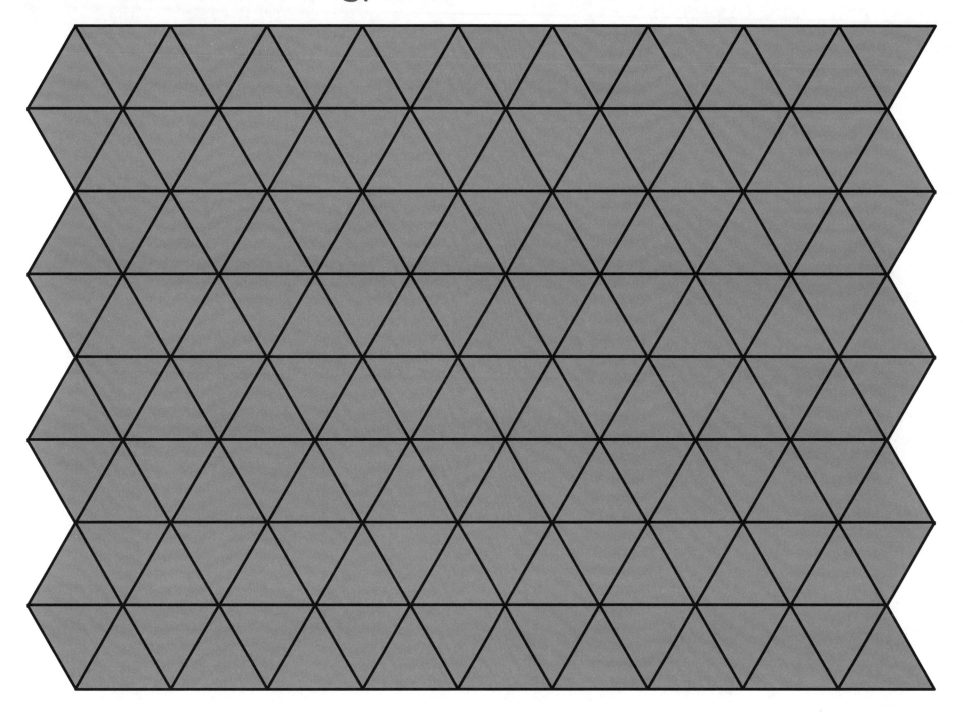

My Starfish 100 Chart

1	2	3	4	5	6	7	8	9	10
11	12	13	14	15	16	17	8	19	20
21	22	23	24	25	26	27	28	29	30
31	32	33	34	35	36	37	38	39	40
41	42	43	44	45	46	47	48	49	50
51	52	53	54	55	56	57	58	59	60
61	62	63	64	65	66	67	68	69	70
71	72	73	74	75	76	77	78	79	80
81	82	83	84	85	86	87	88	89	90
91	92	93	94	95	96	97	98	99	100